Music Making

IN THE ELEMENTARY SCHOOL

Gerald Burakoff and Lawrence Wheeler

For Liz and Sonya

TABLE OF CONTENTS

Foreword	A
Preface	B
Hand signals	C
The Recorder	D
Hush-A Bye	1
The Angel Band	2
Merrily We Roll Along	3
The Bridge of Avignon	4
A Hole In The Bucket	5
Hot Cross Buns	6
Old Brass Wagon	7
Swing Low, Sweet Chariot	8
The Capucine	9
Sleep, Baby, Sleep	10
Turn the Glasses Over	11
Looby Loo	12
I Have Pretty Flowers	13
'Liza Jane	14
Skip to My Lou	15
Sally, Go 'Round the Stars	16
Three Blind Mice	17
Au Clair de la Lune	18
The Caissons Song	19
Twinkle, Twinkle, Little Star	20
Oh, Susanna!	21
The Lone Star Trail	22
Alouette	23
Hush, Little Baby	24
Row, Row, Row Your Boat	25
The Marines' Hymn	26
Are You Sleeping?	27
Polly Wolly Doodle	28
Chorale	29
Billy Boy	30
Sweet Betsy From Pike	31
Du, Du, Liegst Mir Im Herzen	32
Fingering Chart for Soprano Recorder	33

Foreword

Perhaps the most important contribution of the curriculum reform movement during the past 20 years has been the narrowing of the gap between a subject as it was taught in school and the subject as it actually existed outside of the school. In every subject attempts have been and are being made to teach children about the subject as it really is, and to involve them in the processes which are characteristic of and basic to the subject.

While music making has always been an accepted activity in elementary schools, too much of the music used has been only minimally musical and the childrens' involvement has often been academic and unexciting. If music making is to satisfy curriculum reform principles, children must be helped to deal with rich and challenging music, to develop musicianly skills through their contact with satisfying music, and to become more deeply involved with expressive music through their growing mastery of musical techniques and processes.

Music Making in the Elementary School, by Burakoff and Wheeler, is a living example that the best principles of effective teaching and learning can be translated into an actual course of study in music. Using the most musical of simple instruments - the recorder - along with the voice and other classroom instruments; adapting several of the more useful Orff and Kodaly techniques; providing learnable yet richly musical materials as the basis for study; involving the children in progressively more sophisticated musical settings which satisfy aesthetically at the same time that they challenge technically, all add up to an approach which is sound pedagogically and genuine musically. The careful, explicit directions will be a boon to the classroom teacher and a joy to the music specialist. The enrichment activities allow for flexing of musical muscles, while the basic activities provide a strong common curriculum.

That materials of this sort are being developed is a hopeful sign that the music education profession is growing in maturity and relevance. It is to be hoped that full advantage will be taken of this thoughtful and intelligent approach. Children deserve materials of excellence in every subject. *Music Making in the Elementary School* is an important addition to such material in the subject of music.

Bennett Reimer, Professor of Music
Director of Music Education
Case Western Reserve University
Cleveland, Ohio

PREFACE

The book is designed to cover one year of work. The amount of time used to complete the material in it should ultimately depend upon the age and background of the children, and the number and length of music periods in the school. The book can readily be adapted to meet individual teaching situations. Proceed slowly, and introduce one new step at a time. Do not hesitate to review, and spend as much time as is necessary on any of the suggested procedures.

The bell parts may be played on any tuned percussion instrument, for example, chime bars, melody bells, resonator bells, zylophone, or glockenspiel. It is advisable to mix and use as many of the instruments that are available for any given bell part.

The percussion parts may be performed on any rhythm instruments found in the elementary school of today. Feel free to make substitutions for the percussion instruments suggested in the orchestrations.

The suggested chords may be played on piano, guitar, ukelele, or autoharp.

Create introductions as a means of establishing pitch and tempo, and as a cue for children to begin playing and singing.

Hand signals have been used successfully for many years in the field of music education. They were first introduced in England by John Curwen and used most recently by Zoltan Kodaly in Hungary and the Orff Schulwerk classes in Salzburg. Although there are slight variations in the way different people use the hand signals, the approach is basically the same. Hand signals employ both physical and visual responses and have an appeal that is effective with children.

The authors are particularly indebted to Dr. Bennett Reimer of Case Western Reserve University who provided a Foreword; Robert D. Townsend who read and criticized the manuscript; Frank E. Burke for his educational suggestions; Sonya Burakoff for original lyrics and help with orchestrations; Elizabeth Wheeler for typing the manuscript; Dr. Mieczyslaw Kolinski for his musical suggestions; and Harold Newman for his interest and enthusiasm.

Gerald Burakoff

Lawrence Wheeler

March 1968

HAND SIGNALS

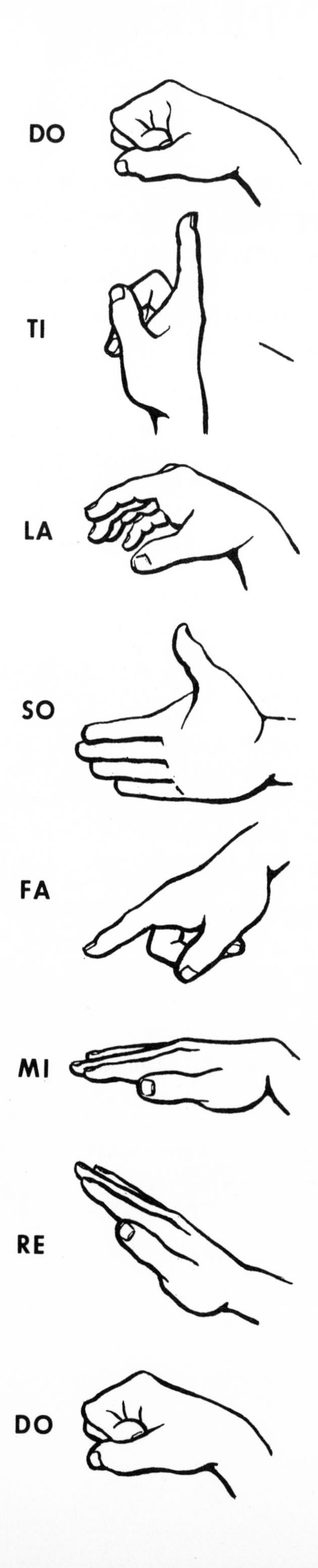

THE RECORDER

A. Recorder In The Elementary Classroom

The recorder is an instrument possessing qualities which make it excellent for use in the elementary music classroom. These qualities are:

1. Ease of playing in the beginning stages.
2. A lack of embouchure problem.
3. Diatonic playing requiring a minimum of technique.
4. Excellent tone quality and intonation.
5. Range of two octaves and a minor third, including all chromatics.
6. A dynamic level well suited for blending with the human voice.

B. Important Points To Stress From the Beginning

1. You should sit erectly, look straight ahead, and hold the recorder at a forty-five degree angle to the body.
2. Fingers should be curved and relaxed. Cover the holes with the cushions of the fingers.
3. The left hand is always on top.
4. You should place the recorder partly over the edge of the lower lip. Bring the upper lip down and the corners of the mouth forward. Teeth should never touch the mouthpiece.
5. You should play in a soft and legato manner most of the time. Go smoothly from one note to the other while still tonguing. Think of the word "daah" when beginning a note.

C. Additional Information

1. The soprano recorder sounds an octave higher than notated.
2. The German and English fingering systems are basically the same. The differences occur in fingering the F and F♯ for the soprano recorder.
3. Recorders should be cleaned with a swab or chamois after each playing session.

INTRODUCING THE RECORDER AND LEARNING THE NOTE B

Children should know this song before this experience is introduced.

A. Suggested Procedure:

1. Discuss the game called "Follow the Leader." This can be related to the echo (answering back).
2. Play "Follow the Leader" with the class. Clap the [rhythm] rhythmic pattern and have the class clap it back on your signal.
3. Maintain a steady rhythm and continue the above procedure with the following patterns:

4. Distribute the recorders and discuss the following:
   a. Name of the instrument *(Soprano Recorder)*.
   b. How the recorder is held
   c. The sound it makes and how the sound is produced
   d. Number of holes and the placement of them on the recorder

5. Show the class how to hold the recorder and play the note "B".

6. Play 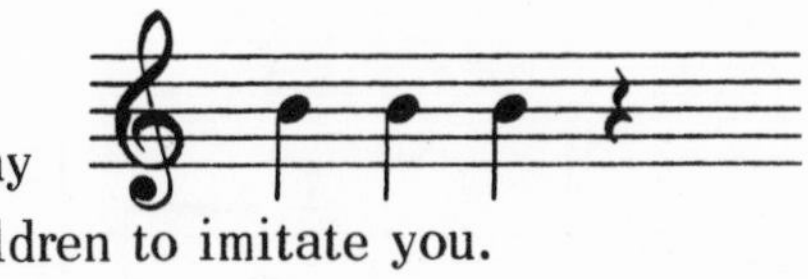 on your recorder. On the fourth count, give the cue for the children to imitate you.

7. Play "B" in various rhythmic combinations and have the children imitate you. For example:

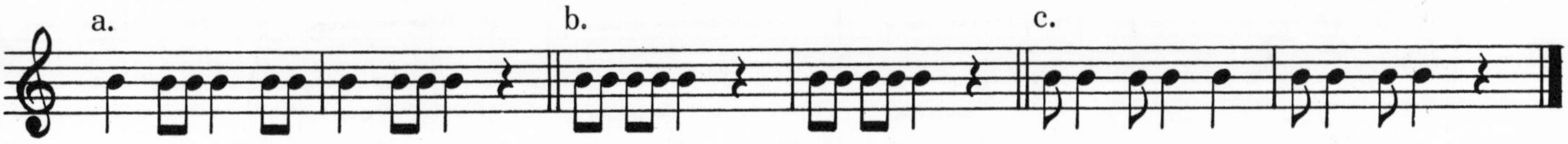

8. Review the song *Hush A Bye*. The children should sing the melody as you play the recorder part.

9. Have the children open their books to page 4 and follow the recorder part as you play. Help the children discover that the note you are playing is written on the third line of the staff and is called "B".

10. Divide the class into two groups. Have one group play the recorder part while the other group sings the melody. Then alternate the groups.

11. Sing the first line of the bell part with the vowel *oo* or *ah*. Show the pitch direction of the bell part with your hands or use the hand signals. Have the children repeat what you have done. Illustrate the skip between the first two notes on the board:

12. Let several children try to play the first line of the bell part on the bells. (Note: It is often helpful to hold the bells so that the lowest note is at waist level and the top note is at approximately shoulder level. This helps to identify the pitch direction of high and low.)

13. Explain to the class that this bell part fits nicely with *Hush A Bye*. Select one child to play the bell part as you sing the first line of the melody.

14. Divide the class into singers and recorder players. Have them play the recorder part and sing the melody of the first line of the orchestration as one child plays the bells. Have the singers clap the rhythm indicated on the tone block and drum lines. Alternate the groups.

15. Help the children become aware of the repetition of the first and third lines of the bell part. Have the class sing and play the entire song while one child plays only the first and third lines of the bell part.

16. Teach the second line of the bell part in a similar manner as above.

17. Add the percussion instruments and have the class sing and play the complete orchestration.

B. Enrichment:

1. Let a small group sing the bell part with the vowel *oo* accompanied by the bells. This can serve as an effective introduction to part singing.

2. Clap 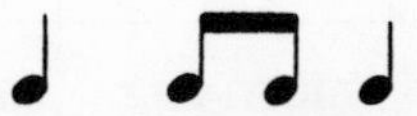 as a simple rhythm accompaniment to the singing.

3. Have the class create a percussion part as an accompaniment.

4. Emphasize the correct recorder tone production.

The Angel Band

A FURTHER EXPERIENCE WITH THE NOTE B 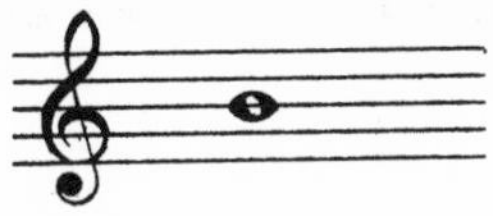

A. Suggested Procedure:

1. Have the class clap a steady ♩ ♩ rhythmic pattern. As the class continues to clap, tell them what you are going to do. Then, sing or play *Angel Band* on the recorder as the class claps.

2. Continue the above procedure, changing to a ♩ ♫ rhythmic pattern.

3. Teach the words of the song. Have the children sing the words as they clap the ♩ ♫ rhythmic pattern.

4. Divide the class into two groups. Have one group sing the melody while the other group plays "B" on their recorders for the first count of every measure of the first three staves. The two groups should sing and clap ♩ ♫ on the fourth and fifth staves. Alternate the groups.

5. Select one child to play 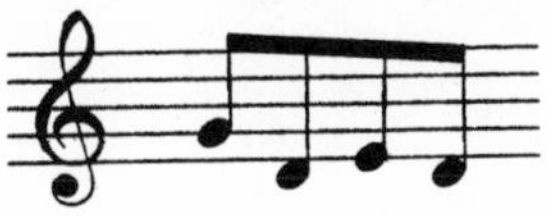 on the bells.

6. Have one child begin the ostinato bell pattern. Have the above two groups of singers and players begin on the teacher's signal. Discontinue the recorder and bell playing on the fourth and fifth staves. The two groups should then sing and clap.

7. Draw 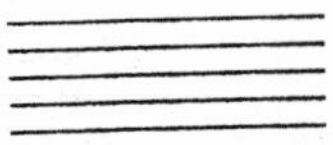 on the board. Ask the children what you drew *(five lines and four spaces)*.

8. Write the treble clef symbol on the staff and have the children identify it. Write "B" on the staff and have the children identify it as the note which is on the middle or third line of the staff.

9. Add the percussion instruments. Have the class sing and play the complete orchestration.

B. Enrichment:

1. Teach another bell part 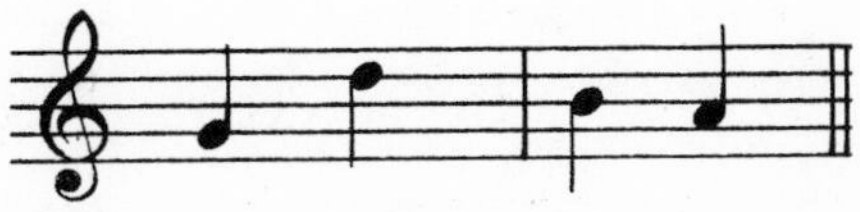 to accompany the singing and playing.

2. Have the class create different rhythmic accompaniments.

3. Have the children sing the bell part and use hand signals. The bell part can be used as a second voice part.

Merrily We Roll Along

America

Recorder

Voice (Melody)

Bells

Tone Block

Drum

G
Mer - ri - ly we roll a - long,

D7
roll a - long,

G
roll a - long,

Mer - ri - ly we

G
roll a - long,

D7
On the deep blue

G
sea.

LEARNING THE NOTE A

A. Suggested Procedure:

1. Play "Follow the Leader" with the class. Tell them to watch and listen carefully and play exactly what you play. Play the following, and on the fourth count give the children the signal to imitate you.

2. Prepare a chart or write the following on the board: (Note: Many teachers believe that the lines and spaces of the staff should be introduced only when needed. Since children are using only two notes, only one line and one space are necessary here. However, if desired, the notation can be used on the regular staff.

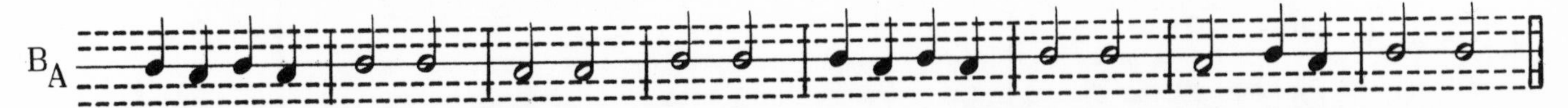

   a. Explain to the children that they know "B" is written on the third line. Then explain that the note just below "B" is called "A." Point to the chart or the board as the children read the note names and finger them on their recorders.
   b. Play the above tune on the recorder. Ask for several volunteers to play it.
   c. Have the class play the tune on their recorders. Tell the children this is the recorder part to *Merrily We Roll Along.*

3. Ask the children who know the song *Merrily We Roll Along* to sing it with you as they clap 𝅗𝅥 𝅗𝅥 (drum part).

4. Divide the class. Have one group play the recorder part as the other group sings and claps 𝅗𝅥 𝅗𝅥. Alternate the groups.

5. Write Tone block / Drum on the board.
   a. Ask for several volunteers to clap the tone block part.
   b. Have the class play and sing *Merrily We Roll Along* as several children clap the tone block part.
   c. Divide the class. One group will clap the tone block part, the other will clap the drum part as they sing the song. If desired, the teacher can select one child in each group to play the rhythm instruments (drum and tone block) and serve as the leader for his group.

6. Hold the bells with the bottom at waist level and play the bell part. Ask the class to sing with the vowel *oo* and show the melodic direction with their hands or hand signals as you play the bell part.

7. Ask for volunteers to play the bell part as the class sings the song and uses hand signals.

8. Select one child to play the bells. Have the class play and sing the entire orchestration.

B. Enrichment:

1. Teach the clap / stamp *patchen** ostinato to accompany the song.

2. Teach snap / clap / r. knee / l. knee / stamp as another *patchen* ostinato to the song.

3. Teach the children the autoharp accompaniment.

* *Patchen* is a term used in the Orff-Schulwerk to describe rhythmic accompaniments which include stamping, knee patting, clapping, and finger snapping. The notation appearing on the different lines does not indicate pitch, but is related to the use of different parts of the body. Practice the examples slowly at the beginning. After a few times, they become easy and very enjoyable for the children.

The Bridge of Avignon

FURTHER EXPERIENCE WITH THE NOTE A

A. Suggested Procedure:

1. Have the class echo your speech pattern (below) as they rhythmically clap hands and pat knees.
   a. Establish a steady clap - pat quarter note rhythm and say the speech pattern of the first line as:

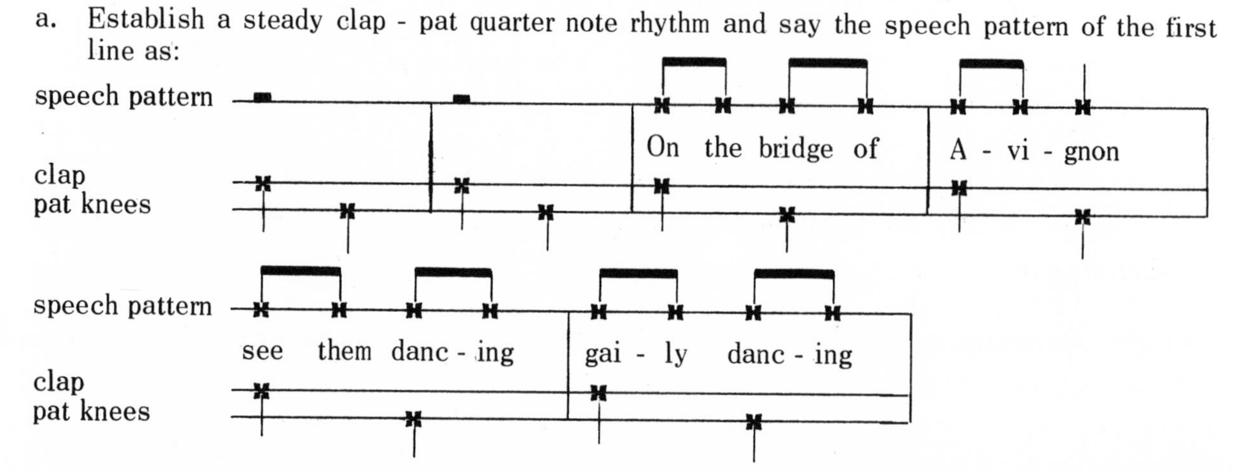

   b. Have the children echo you upon your signal. (Note: It is essential to maintain a steady uninterrupted rhythm throughout this type of activity.)
   c. Continue the word rhythms of the song, as outlined above, line by line, in the same way.
   d. Now say the words for the entire song as the children clap and pat.
2. To determine whether the class knows the correct word rhythms, have the children clap the note values of the words of the song.

3. Establish the children clapping and patting in a steady rhythm. Tell them:
   a. To say the first word of the song aloud upon your signal.
   b. To silently think the rest of the words in the song as they continue clapping and patting.
   c. To say the last word aloud.
   d. Repeat the above procedure two or three times.
4. Play the melody on the recorder as the children accompany you by clapping and patting.
5. Ask for volunteers to sing the song with you as you play the melody on the recorder.
6. Begin clapping ♩ ♫ with the class. As they continue clapping, play the second line of the melody as an introduction. Play the melody as the children sing and clap the accompaniment.
   (Note: Singing one rhythmic pattern and clapping another requires a strong physical feeling for rhythm. Children need many opportunities for experiences of this type to develop rhythmic stability. Have a rhythmically secure child play the ♩ ♫ pattern on the tone block and serve as a leader for the class.)
7. Write the following on the board or chart:

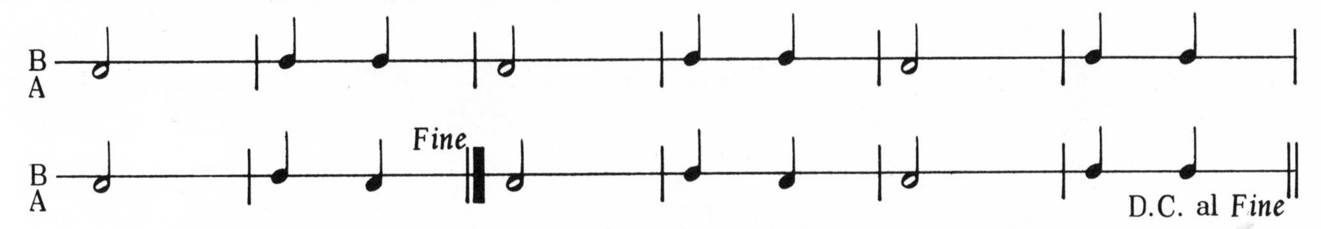

   a. Remind the children that in *Merrily We Roll Along* they learned that the note "B" was on the line and the note "A" was in the space below. Play the recorder part (shown above) and then ask volunteers to play it with you.
   b. Have the entire class play the recorder part as you or one child points to the notes on the board or chart.
   c. Explain that this is an accompanying part to *The Bridge of Avignon*. Divide the class. Have one group sing the melody as the other group plays the recorder part. Play and sing the song.
   d. Alternate the groups.
   e. Select one child to play the tone block part (♩ ♫). Sing and play the song.
8. Play the first two lines of the bell part.
9. Ask the children to sing the bell part and show its melodic direction with their hands or hand signals.
10. Ask the class to sing the melody as the teacher plays the first two lines of the bell part. Stress the importance of listening to how the parts fit together.
11. Ask for several volunteers to play the bell part.
12. Play the bell part for the third line. Then let several volunteers play it.
13. Combine the melody, bell, and percussion parts. Play and sing the song.
14. Add the recorder part to the ensemble and play and sing the complete orchestration.

B. Enrichment:

1. As a preparatory activity to part singing, use the words of the song and create a two-part speech round. The second part begins one measure after the first part.
2. Create a percussion part to accompany the speech round.
3. Have a small group of children sing the bell part as a second part.
4. Teach the dance steps below:
   a. Form a double circle, partners facing each other.
   b. Outer circle (boys) moves step-close (♩ ♩) to the right and the inner circle (girls) moves step-close to the left (first 8 measures).
   c. On the bottom line of the song, have the boys bow to their partners as indicated in the text.
   d. Repeat b. above, in reverse direction for the D.C. *al Fine*.

A Hole in the Bucket

Americ

Recorder

Voice (Melody)

There's a hole in the buck - et, dear Li - za, dear

Bells

Tone Block

Triangle

LEARNING THE NOTE G

A. Suggested Procedure:

1. Play various one-measure combinations of "B", "A", "G". Have the children echo or play-back the following patterns:

(Note: In all play or clap-backs, it is important to maintain a steady rhythm.)

2. Write 

on the board or large cardboard.

   a. Ask the children the name of the first note. Establish that it is "G". Show the recorder fingering for "G". Recall that the other notes are "A" and "B".
   b. Play the example shown above on the recorder.
   c. Tell the class to listen and tell you the number of times this pattern is heard in *A Hole in the Bucket.* Play these three notes again to establish the pattern and then play the song.
   d. To clarify, play the song again and have the children raise their hands each time the pattern is heard.
3. Ask the children to find this pattern in the melody line in their song books.
4. Tell the class to play the three-note pattern when it occurs and to sing the words of the song when they are not playing. Play and sing the song.
5. Ask the children to tell you the note value written for the triangle part. *(dotted half note)* Explain that a dotted half note gets three counts. Count 1-2-3 over and over. Strike the triangle on the first count and pulse the second and third counts silently in the air. Repeat as children clap-pulse-pulse with you.
6. Identify the first count of the tone block part as a quarter rest. Pulse in the air on one and strike the tone block on 2 and 3. Children should pulse, clap, clap with you.
7. Combine the triangle and tone block parts.
8. Develop a plan for playing and singing:
   a. Divide the class into singers, tone block, triangle, and recorder players.
   b. Have the triangle and the tone block players play a two-measure introduction.
   c. The recorder players and the singers should begin on the third count of the second measure of the introduction.
9. Write 

on the board.

   a. Have the class identify the names of the notes.
   b. Call attention to the correct use of the right and left hands for bell playing.
   c. Have the children sing these notes as they play imaginary bells in the air.
10. Select one child to play the bell part as the class sings the song.
11. Teach the recorder part.
12. Combine all the parts. Play and sing the complete orchestration.

B. Enrichment:

1. Teach the snap / clap / stamp patchen ostinato.
2. Create an introduction, interlude, and coda for the recorder with various combinations of the notes "B", "A", "G".

Hot Cross Buns

Children's Song

FURTHER EXPERIENCE WITH THE NOTE G

The teacher may find it desirable to develop this experience in two class periods rather than one to make certain the children absorb the musical concepts.

A. Suggested Procedure:

1. Begin clapping your hands and patting your knees in a steady rhythm, then have the children join you. As they clap, play *Hot Cross Buns* on your recorder.
2. Have the children identify the title of the song.
3. Have the children play the notes "B", "A", "G" on the words "Hot cross buns" as they appear in the song. They should sing all the other words.
4. Ask the class if the notes they played are close together or far apart (step or skip).
5. Ask the children how many different notes are used in the song. *(three)*.
6. Draw ——— on the board.

   a. Ask the children what you drew *(two lines)*.
   b. Have the children discover the space between the lines. Establish the idea of step as a line to a space or a space to a line.
   c. Using the recorder fingering pattern as a visual aid, establish the direction of the melodic line for *Hot Cross Buns*.

7. Write [staff] on the board.

   Hot cross buns

   a. Have the children use circles to place the notes on the staff for the words "Hot cross buns." Play your recorder to guide the children in notating the "B", "A", "G".
   b. The third line can now be identified as "B", the second space as "A", and the second line as "G".

8. Ask for volunteers to step the notes values for the words, "Hot cross buns."

   step step step-bend
   "Hot cross buns"

   a. Relate the steps to quarter notes and the step-bends to half notes.

   b. Show the notation for the first three notes as:

   B
   G
   Hot cross buns

   c. Tell the children to clap and count "one" for each quarter note and clap and pull hands up and count "one-two" for each half note. There are other ways to count quarter and half notes:

   one two three-four
   tah tah tah - ah

(Note: The teacher should consistently use one counting system throughout all suggested experiences.)

9. Have the class clap, count, and sing:

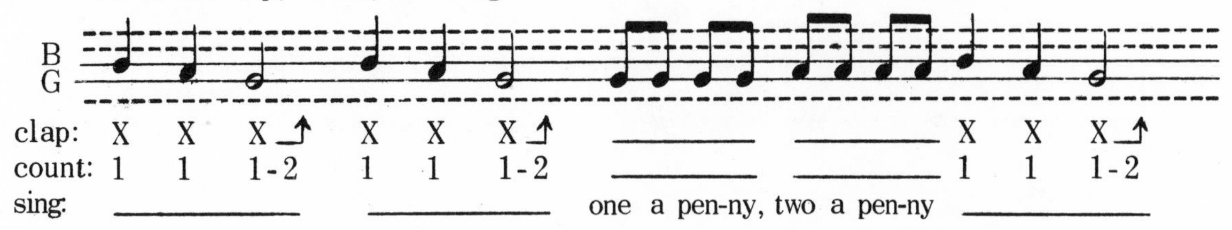

10. Select one child to step the words "Hot cross buns" and another child to step "one a penny, two a penny". Have the class sing the song as the two children step these word patterns.
11. Discuss with the class that the words "one a penny, two a penny" are related to running steps.

   a. Relate these running steps to eighth notes and notate as follows:

   b. Tell the children that each pair of eighth notes may be counted "one-and", There are other ways to count eighth notes:

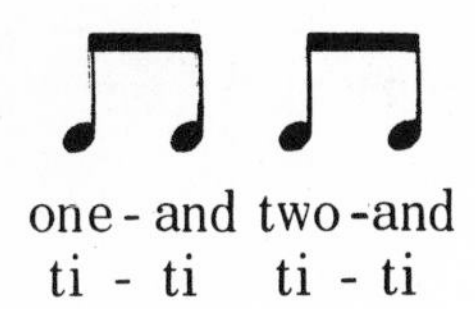

12. Have the children clap and count the word rhythms of the song.
13. Write

on the board.

   a. Ask the class to clap and count the rhythm.
   b. Point to the "G" line and guide the class to discover the note names for "C" and "D".
   c. Ask for several volunteers to play this on the bells.
14. Select one child to play the bell accompaniment as the class sings and plays the melody on their recorders.

B. Enrichment:

1. Teach the recorder part.
2. Teach the percussion part.
3. Create an introduction and interlude for the recorder and use the notes "B", "A", "G".
4. Teach the children to play the autoharp chords as an accompaniment to their singing and playing.
5. Another bell part could be:

Old Brass Wagon

FURTHER EXPERIENCE WITH THE NOTE G

A. Suggested procedure:

1. Tell the class you will clap a rhythmic pattern and they are to clap it back when you signal.
   a. Clap the first two measures of rhythm of the melody and have the children clap-back to you.
   b. Continue the two-measure clap-backs for the remainder of the song.
   c. Extend the clap-backs to four-measure phrases.
   d. Extend the clap-backs to the entire song.
2. Explain to the class that the clap-backs are the word rhythms to the song, *Old Brass Wagon.*
3. Go over the words of the song with the class.
4. Establish a steady (stamp clap stamp clap) rhythm and play or sing the song.
5. Select one child to play the drum part as the rest of the class sings and stamp-claps.
6. Have the children look at the first four measures of the melody to see if there are any short phrases they can play on their recorders. (First measure, "circle to the left", the note "G". Third measure, "circle to the left", the note "A".)
7. Have the class play the "circle to the left" on their recorders and sing the words "the Old Brass Wagon" for the first four measures of the song.
8. Follow the same procedure above, 6 and 7, for the last four measures of the melody. (Play "B's" on "circle to the left".)
9. Write on the board.
   a. Have the children identify the note values (*eighths and quarters*).
   b. Clap the pattern and have the class clap back as you point to the notes on the board.
   c. Sing the song and use the rhythmic pattern as an introduction and accompaniment.
   d. Divide the class. One group should sing the melody and clap the rhythmic accompaniment while the other group plays the "circle to the left" (notes "G", "A", "B") on their recorders.
10. Write B G on the board.
    a. Have the children name the notes. (If they do not know the note "D", point to the "B" line and guide the children to discover the note "D")
    b. Ask for several volunteers to play the pattern on the bells.
11. Show the class how to play B G on the bells and let several children try.
12. Select children to play the two bell parts. Divide the class into singer-clappers and recorder players. Play and sing the song.
13. Teach the recorder part.
14. Combine all the parts. Play and sing the complete orchestration.

B. Enrichment:

1. Create an introduction and coda to the song for bells and percussion.
2. Create other words for the song ("circle to the right", "jumping up and down").
3. Explain to the class that improvising means making up their own music. Illustrate by playing the following example or one of your own choice:

   a. Ask for several volunteers to make up a short piece on their recorders using the notes "B", "A", "G".
   b. Use the children's improvisations as interludes between repetitions of the song. Continue only the rhythmic accompaniment during the improvisations.
4. Sing *Old Brass Wagon* as a two-part round. The second part should enter when the first part reaches the fifth measure.
5. Create a dance for the song.

Swing Low, Sweet Chariot

LEARNING THE NOTE C

Children should know this song before this experience is introduced.

A. Suggested Procedure:

1. Ask the children to say *doo, doo, doo* softly and smoothly.
2. Show the recorder fingering for the note "C".
3. Ask the children to echo what you play. Play the note "C" with the following rhythms:

4. With the notes "C" and "A", have the children imitate you on the following play-backs.

5. Write on the board

   B
   G

   a. Ask for volunteers to clap and count the rhythm.
   b. Ask the children to identify the note names and finger them on their recorders.
   c. Ask for several volunteers to play this melodic pattern.
   d. Have the entire class play the pattern. If necessary, point to the notes. Tell children this repeated pattern is called an ostinato.
   e. Ask the children how many times this ostinato appears in the recorder part.
6. Divide the class into recorder players and singers.
7. Have the class sing the song as you play ostinato on the bells.

8. Ask for several volunteers to play the bell part.
9. Select one child to play the bell part. Divide the class into recorder players and singers. Play and sing the song.

B. Enrichment:

1. Sing *Swing Low* as a round. The second part should enter one measure after the first part.
2. A more difficult bell ostinato which can be used is:
3. Select a small group of children to sing the recorder part or the bell part as a second voice part.
4. Teach the percussion accompaniment to the song.
5. Another patchen accompaniment can be: clap stamp

The Capucine

English Lyric by
Sonya Burakoff

French

FURTHER EXPERIENCE WITH THE NOTE C 

A. Suggested Procedure:

1. Write ♩ ♫ ♩ ♫ on the board.
   a. Ask the children to identify the note values (*quarters and eighths*).
   b. Ask the children how they clapped these note values for Hot Cross Buns (*"one" for every quarter note, and "one-and" for two eighth notes*).
   c. Have the children clap and count this pattern softly as you play the melody on your recorder.

2. Have the children sing the melody of *Capucine* with syllables. Direct them with hand signals.

3. Have the children open their books and clap and count the rhythm of the melody as you play it on your recorder.

4. Select one child to play the tone block. Have the child play two measures of ♩ ♫ ♩ ♫ as an introduction and accompaniment as the class sings the song.

5. Have the entire class sing the song and clap the tone block part.

6. Ask the children to tell you how many different notes are used in the melody (*four*).

7. Have the class name the notes as they appear in the melody and finger them on their recorders.

8. Ask for volunteers to play the first four measures of the melody with you on their recorders as the other children finger the notes silently.

9. Select one child to play the tone block part. Divide the class into singers and recorder players. Play and sing the melody with the tone block accompaniment.

10. Have the class clap and count the recorder part.

11. Select several children to play the recorder part as the class claps and counts.

12. Let the entire class play the recorder part.

13. Divide the class into: recorder players playing the recorder part; recorder players playing the melody; and singers singing the melody. Play and sing the song.

B. Enrichment:

1. Teach the bell part.
2. Another bell ostinato which can be used is: 
3. Create a rhythm accompaniment with different percussion instruments.
4. Encourage rhythmic and melodic improvisations for interludes.

Sleep, Baby, Sleep

English Lyric by
Sonya Burakoff

Germ

FURTHER EXPERIENCE WITH THE NOTE C 

A. Suggested Procedure:

1. Ask the children to follow the melody as you play it on your recorder. Tell the class you will stop at different places, and they should tell you where you stopped. Play the melody several times.
2. Show the class how to play the on the triangle.

   1 - 2 strike - pulse and 1 - 2 - dot strike - pulse - pulse
3. Teach the words to the song.
4. Have the class sing the melody as one child plays the triangle part.
5. Write the following on the board or large cardboard:

   a. Ask the class to clap and count the rhythm. (If necessary, review counting the quarter rests as "rest".)
   b. Have the children identify the names of the notes.
   c. Play the above example on the bells and sing the note names as the class claps the rhythm.
   d. Have the class sing the note names as you play the bells.
   e. Ask for several volunteers to play the bells as the class sings the note names.
   f. Select one child to play the bells and another child to play the triangle. Divide the class. Have one group sing the bell part while the other group sings the melody. Play and sing the song.
6. Help the children become aware that the recorder part uses only four notes, "C", "B", "A", "G".
7. Write B G on the board.

   Have the children play their recorders as you point to the notes. Point to the notes in the sequence and the rhythm in which they appear in the recorder part.
8. Now have the children play the recorder part written in their books.
9. Combine all the parts. Play and sing the complete orchestration.

B. Enrichment:

1. Create an introduction, interlude, and coda for the recorder and rhythm instruments.
2. Create a melodic improvisation for the recorder in the following way:
   a. Explain to the children that they can make up many melodies with the notes "C", "B", "A", "G" in different combinations.
   b. Illustrate by playing

   as an example of improvisation.

Turn the Glasses Over

America

LEARNING THE NOTE D

A. Suggested Procedure:

1. Write on the board.

B
G

   a. Ask the children the names of the notes.
   b. Guide them to discover the fourth line "D". Show the recorder fingering for "D".
   c. Ask for several volunteers to play the "D", "A", "B", "G" pattern on their recorders.
   d. Have the entire class play this pattern as you play or sing *Turn the Glasses Over.*

2. Use as a clap-back.
   a. Ask the class how they would count this rhythmic pattern. Clap it as many times as necessary until the children establish that it is counted: "one, one, one-and, one-and."
   b. Ask for one volunteer to write this rhythmic pattern on the board.
   c. Divide the class. Have one group play the recorder part while the other group claps as you sing the melody. Alternate the groups.

3. Write this bell part on the board.

   a. Have the children identify the note names for the top bell part.
   b. Select one child to play this on the bells.
   c. Repeat *a.* and *b.* for the low bell part.
   d. Combine both bell parts.
4. Divide the class into clappers, recorder players, bell players, and singers.
   a. Start with a two-measure clapping introduction
   b. The recorder players enter at the third measure while the clapping continues.
   c. The bell players enter at the fifth measure.
   d. The singers enter at the seventh measure.

B. Enrichment:
1. Create a dance to accompany the singing.
2. Teach the drum part.
3. Teach the children to play as another bell part.

D
B
G

4. Teach as another patchen accompaniment.

clap
r. knee
l. knee
stamp

5. Create melodic improvisations between the verses with the notes "B", "A", "G", "D".
6. Have the children play the melodies of *Hush A Bye* and *Merrily We Roll Along* on their recorders.

FURTHER EXPERIENCE WITH THE NOTE D

A. Suggested Procedure:

1. Begin with the following rhythmic warm up (clapping must be continuous throughout):
   a. Clap and count quarter notes as "one, one, one, one". Then have the children join you.
   b. Tell the class to clap and count eighth notes on your signal.
   c. Tell the class to clap and count half notes on your signal.
   d. Follow the above procedure and vary the clapping of quarters, eighths, and half notes.

2. Write (3) on the board. Have the children clap and count the triplets with you.
   tri - pl - ty

(Note: There are several other ways in which (3) can be counted: tri-p-let; one-and-dah; one-two-three. One counting system must be selected and consistently used throughout all suggested experiences.)

3. Follow the procedure suggested above (1), adding the triplets.

4. Have the children clap back the following rhythms.:

a. b. c.

d. e.

5. Ask the class to tell you the time signature for *Looby Loo.*
6. The children should understand that in 6/8 meter there are six counts to a measure and an eighth note gets one count.
7. Ask the children to identify the following note values found in the orchestration by saying the word rhythms and clapping.

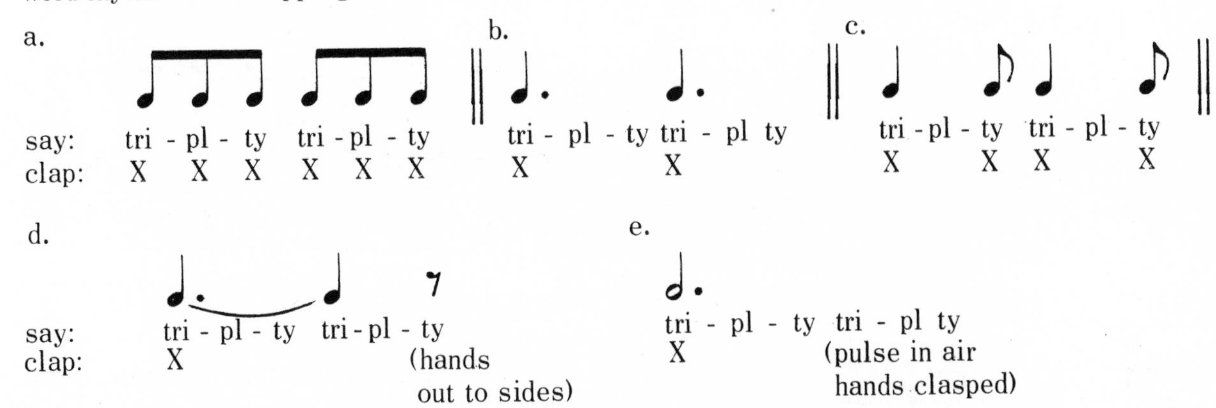

8. Have the children clap and count various combinations of the above 6/8 patterns.
9. Ask for several volunteers to clap and count the rhythm of the melody.
10. Have the entire class clap and count the rhythm of the melody. (If they have difficulty, write the rhythm on the board and guide the children by pointing and saying the proper word rhythms.)
11. Have the children sing the melody as you play it on your recorder.
12. Write the following on the board:

say: tri - pl - ty tri - pl - ty tri - pl - ty tri - pl - ty
clap: X X X X X X X

   a. Have the class clap and count this pattern.
   b. Select one child to play the pattern on the tone block as the class sings and claps.

13. Write on the board. Have the children play their recorders as you point to the notes. Point to the notes in the sequence and the rhythm in which they appear in the recorder part.
14. Have the children clap and count the rhythm for the recorder part.
15. Have the children play the recorder part.
16. Divide the class into two groups. Have one group sing the song while the other group plays the recorder part. Use the tone block pattern as an accompaniment.

B. Enrichment:

1. Teach the children the bell part.
2. Teach the children the drum part.
3. Create an introduction, interlude, and coda for rhythm instruments.
4. Play and sing the song and have different children improvise between repetitions of the song.
5. Teach the autoharp accompaniment.
6. Relate the time signature concept to other songs in the book.

I Have Pretty Flowers

Lyric by
Sonya Burakoff

Fren

FURTHER EXPERIENCE WITH THE NOTE D

A. Suggested Procedure:

1. Begin clapping the pattern at a moderate tempo. Invite the children to join you.

2. Tell the children to continue clapping as you sing *I Have Pretty Flowers*.

3. Teach the children to sing the song as they clap the accompaniment.

4. Write on the board.

   a. Play this short phrase on your recorder.

   b. Have the children count how many times the phrase occurs as you play the recorder part *(four)*.

   c. Have the children sing the phrase each time it occurs as you play the recorder part.

   d. Ask the children where the phrase appears in the recorder part *(first and last four measures)*.

   e. Have the children mark an A at the beginning of the first and last four measures.

5. Have the class discover that measures 5–8 of the recorder part consists of two two-measure phrases. Mark measure five with a B.

6. Make the children aware of the ABA form.

7. Divide the class into two groups. Have one group sing the melody with the clapping accompaniment while the other group plays the first and last 4 measures of the recorder part, and sings measures 5–8.

8. Have the class play the entire recorder part.

9. Divide the class. Play and sing the song.

B. Enrichment:

1. Encourage the children to play the melody on their recorders (with or without music).

2. Teach the bell part, relating it to the ABA concept.

3. Create an introduction, interlude, and coda for rhythm instruments or recorders.

4. Teach the percussion part for the suggested instruments.

'Liza Jane

American

LEARNING THE NOTE F

Children should know this song before this experience is introduced.

A. Suggested Procedure:

1. Play the following on your recorder and have the children echo you:

2. Have the children identify the names of the notes in the recorder part. Guide them to discover the note "F" and show them the recorder fingering.

3. Ask for volunteers to play the recorder part as the class claps a steady quarter note rhythmic accompaniment. To avoid confusion, determine the length of a clapping introduction.

4. Have the entire class play the recorder part. If they have difficulty, write D B G on the board and point to the notes to be played or review above (1.).

5. Divide the class. Have one group play the recorder part while the other group sings and claps.

6. Ask the children to look at the bell part and name the first note ("F"). By this time, the children should be aware of the five-line staff and the names of the lines and spaces.

7. Show the children how to play the bell part. Give several children an opportunity to play the bell part as the class sings and plays the song.

B. Enrichment:

1. Teach the drum and tone block accompaniment.

2. Encourage the children to create rhythmic and melodic improvisations between verses.

3. Teach snap / clap / pat knees / stamp to accompany the singing.

4. Have the children sing the recorder part on *oo* for two-part singing.

Skip to My Lou
America
Recorder
Voice (Melody)
Bells
Tone Block
Tambourine
F C7
Flies in the but-ter-milk shoo, fly, shoo. Flies in the but-ter-milk
shoo, fly, shoo. Flies in the but-ter-milk shoo, fly, shoo. Skip to my Lou, my
dar - ling. Skip, skip, skip to my Lou, Skip, skip,
skip to my Lou, Skip, skip, skip to my Lou, skip to my Lou, my dar - ling.

FURTHER EXPERIENCE WITH THE NOTE F

A. Suggested Procedure:

1. Write ♩ ♫ (sixteenth notes) on the board.
   a. Have the children identify the note values.
   b. Make the children aware of the horizontal lines connecting the eighth and sixteenth notes.
   c. Establish with the class that sixteenth notes are counted (sixteenth notes) one tuh and tuh
2. Write on the board: (rhythm pattern)
   a. Ask for volunteers to clap and count this rhythm.
   b. Have the entire class clap and count. If necessary, help them by pointing to the notes.
3. Tell the children you are going to clap the word rhythms of a familiar song. Clap the word rhythms for *Skip to My Lou* and ask the class if they recognize the song.
4. Have the children sing the song as they clap the word rhythms and step quarter notes.
5. Write  D B G (notes on staff) on the board. Have the children play their recorders as you point to the notes. Point to the notes in the sequence and the rhythm in which they appear in the recorder part.
6. Have the children name the notes of the recorder part as they finger them.
7. Write (rhythm pattern) on the board. Have the class clap this pattern as an accompaniment to their singing.
8. Use two measures of (rhythm pattern) as an introduction. Play and sing the song.

B. Enrichment:

1. Teach the bell part.
2. Create a recorder introduction, interlude and coda with the notes "F", "G", "A", "C".
3. Teach the autoharp chording to accompany the singing.
4. Have the children sing either the recorder part or the bell part with the melody as a two-part singing experience.
5. Create dance steps or use the following:
   a. Form a large double circle, girls on the inside, boys on the outside.
   b. Have the boys clap ♩ ♩ for the first six measures as the girls skip to the right.
   c. On measures 7-8 have everyone clap.
   d. On measures 9-14, the partners should join hands and skip to the left.
   e. In the last two measures, have everyone clap.

Sally, Go 'Round the Stars

English

FURTHER EXPERIENCE WITH THE NOTE F

A. Suggested Procedure:

1. Show the class how to play the bell part. Let several children try as the class claps ♩. ♩.

2. Have the children play-back

3. Write 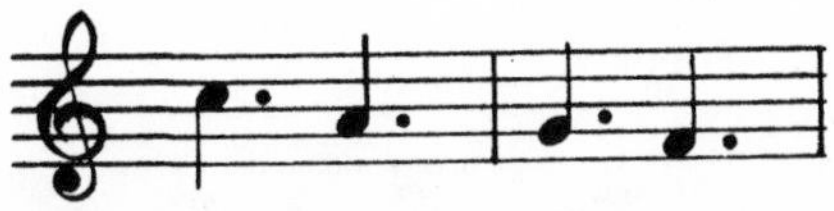 on the board. Ask the class how many times this melodic pattern occurs in the recorder part (*four*).

4. Divide the class into recorder players and bell players.
   a. Start with a four-measure bell introduction.
   b. The recorder players enter at the fifth measure.
   c. You should begin singing the song at the ninth measure as the bells and recorders continue to play.

5. Teach the words of the song.

6. Ask for volunteers to sing the song with you.

7. Have the entire class sing the song.

8. Divide the class into singers, recorder players, and bell players. Play and sing the song.

B. Enrichment:

1. Have the class play the melody on their recorders with or without music.
2. Create dance steps.
3. Teach the percussion part notated in the score.
4. Have the children sing the bell part on *oo* as a second voice part.
5. Create another rhythmic orchestration.

Three Blind Mice

American

LEARNING THE NOTE E

Children should know this song before this experience is introduced.

A. Suggested Procedure:

1. Have the class clap / stamp

When a steady rhythm has been established, have the class sing *Three Blind Mice*.

2. Write the following on the board:

   a. Have the children identify the note names and show them the recorder fingering for the first line "E".
   b. Play one of the examples shown above on your recorder and ask the children which melodic phrase you played.
   c. Have the children play the same phrase on their recorders.
   d. Continue this plan for all the phrases.
3. Have the children play the recorder part.
4. Divide the class into singers and recorder players. Play and sing the song.
5. Write 6/8 ♩ ♪♩ ♪ | ♫♪ ♩ 𝄾 on the board.
   a. Ask the children to count and clap. (If necessary, review *Looby Loo* on page 15.)
   b. Have the children clap this pattern as they sing *Three Blind Mice*.
6. Select one child to play the tone block part. Divide the class into recorder players and singers. Play and sing the song with a four-measure tone block introduction.
7. Have the class sing the song as you play the bell part.
8. Play and sing the entire orchestration as you or one child plays the bell part.

B. Enrichment:

1. Create a rhythmic accompaniment as follows:
   a. Measure 1 through 4 clap: ♩. ♩. | ♩. ♩. | ♩. ♩. | ♩. ♩. ||
   b. Measures 5 through 8 pat knees: ♩. ♩ ♪| ♩. ♩. | ♩. ♩ ♪| ♩. ♩. ||
   c. Measures 9 through 12 snap fingers: ♩. ♩. | ♩. ♩. | ♩. ♩. | ♩. ♩. ||
   d. Last four measures stamp and clap: clap / stamp
2. Divide the class into four groups and do the above as a four-part rhythm round.

Au clair de la lune

FURTHER EXPERIENCE WITH THE NOTE E

A. Suggested Procedure:

1. Write on the board:

   a. Have the children show the pitch direction of this phrase with their hands or hand signals as you play it on your recorder.

   b. Have the children sing this phrase on *oo* as you play it on your recorder.

   c. Play the recorder part and ask the class to tell you the number of times this phrase is heard (*three*).

   d. Play the recorder part again as the class claps the rhythm and one child points to the notes on the board each time the phrase occurs.

   e. Have the children look at the recorder part in their books and draw a bracket and mark A above this phrase each time it occurs: [A]

2. Ask the class the note names for this phrase and have several volunteers play the phrase with you on their recorders.

3. Have the children play the A section of the recorder part each time it occurs.

4. Teach the children the B section (measures 9 - 12). Then play the entire recorder part.

5. Have the children play the recorder part as you sing the melody.

6. Teach the children to sing the song.

7. Teach the bell part emphasizing AABA form.

8. Sing the song with recorder and bell accompaniment.

B. Enrichment:

1. Teach the percussion part.
2. Create a recorder introduction, interlude, and coda.
3. Have the children sing the recorder part with the melody as a part singing experience.
4. Teach snap / clap / stamp as a rhythmic accompaniment.
5. Have the class sing the song and use hand signals.

The Caissons Song

Recorder
Voice (Melody)
Bells
Tone Block
Drum
O-ver hill, o-ver dale, We have hit the dust-y trail, And those cais-sons
In and out, hear them shout: "Coun-ter march and right a-bout," And those cais-sons
roll-ing a-long.
roll-ing a-long.
Then it's hi hi hee! In the Field Ar-til-ler-y,
Sound off your num-bers loud and strong;
And where-e'er you go,
You will al-ways know,
That those cais-sons go roll-ing a-long.

FURTHER EXPERIENCE WITH THE NOTE E

A. Suggested Procedure:

1. Write

on the board.

   a. Have the children clap the rhythm, making definite motions to their sides for the rests.

   b. Have the children become aware of the repeat sign.

   c. Select one child to point to the rhythmic pattern on the board as the class claps.

   d. Sing the song as the class claps the rhythmic accompaniment.

2. Have the children clap the drum part as you sing the song.

3. Divide the class. Have one group clap the tone block part while the other group claps the drum part. Alternate groups.

4. Sing the song as the class claps the tone block part and drum parts.

5. Teach the class to sing the song.

6. Have the children learn the recorder part in eight-measure phrases. Use a chart, the children's book, the blackboard, or play-backs.

7. Divide the class into singers and recorder players. Play and sing the song and use the percussion accompaniment.

B. Enrichment:

1. Teach the bell part.

2. Have the children march and sing the song. If desired, create march formations.

3. Create a percussion introduction for rhythm instruments.

4. Use the first-last word technique suggested in *The Bridge of Avignon.*

Twinkle, Twinkle, Little Star

Children's Son[g]

LEARNING THE NOTE E

A. Suggested Procedure:

1. Have the children sing the song as you play the bell part.
2. Ask the children to identify the note names of the first line of the bell part.
3. Ask for several volunteers to play the first line of the bell part.
4. Ask the class where this phrase occurs again in the bell part (*third line*).
5. Have the class sing the entire song as one child plays the first and third lines of the bell part.
6. Ask the children the note names for the second line of the bell part. Make sure they identify the "F♯".
7. Ask for several volunteers to play the entire bell part as an accompaniment to the class singing.
8. Write on the board.
   a. Have the children identify this note as fourth space "E".
   b. Show the recorder fingering for "E".
   c. Have the children play-back the following:

9. Ask the children to clap the rhythm of the first line of the recorder part. Ask the class where this phrase occurs again (*third line*).
10. Ask for several volunteers to play the first line of the recorder part. If they have difficulty, write

on the board.

Have the children play their recorders as you point to the notes. Point to the notes in the sequence and the rhythm in which they appear in the recorder part.

11. Teach the second line of the recorder part in a similar manner. Then play the entire recorder part.
12. Divide the class into singers and recorder players.
13. Teach the triangle part. Combine all the parts. Play and sing the entire orchestration.

B. Enrichment:

1. Have the children play the melody on their recorders with or without the music.
2. Have a group of children sing either the recorder part or the bell part as a second voice part.
3. Have the class create or improvise an introduction, interlude, and coda for recorder.
4. Teach the autoharp chording.
5. Have the children sing the song as a two-part round. The second part should begin one measure after the first part.
6. Have the class play the melody of *Au Clair de la Lune* on their recorders.

Oh, Susanna!

FURTHER EXPERIENCE WITH THE NOTE E

A. Suggested Procedure:

1. Write  on the board.

    a. Have the children clap and count the rhythm.

    b. Have the children sing syllables, numbers, or letter names, and show the melodic direction with their hands or hand signals.

    c. Have the children play this phrase several times on their recorders.

    d. Play the recorder part and ask the children how many times this two-measure phrase is heard *(three)*.

    e. Play the recorder part again and have children sing the phrase or clap the rhythm each time the phrase is heard.

    f. Have the children open their books and find where this phrase occurs in the recorder part.

2. Have the class play the first four measures of the recorder part.

3. Have the children compare measures 1–4 with 5–8. They should be aware of the slight differences in these two phrases.

4. Have the class play the first eight measures of the recorder part.

5. Review AABA form and sing *Oh, Susanna* as the children play the first eight and last four measures of the recorder part.

6. Teach the recorder part for measures 9–12.

7. Sing *Oh, Susanna* while the children play the recorder part.

8. Write the following on the board:

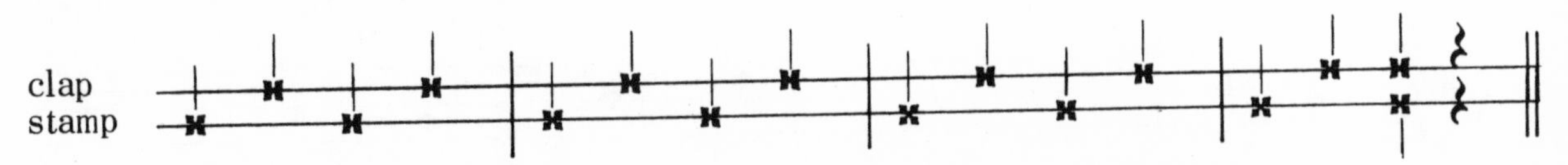

   a. Have the class clap and stamp.
   b. Sing the song as the children continue the rhythmic accompaniment.

9. Teach the children the song.

10. Have the class sing the song with the rhythmic accompaniment above (8).

11. Select children to play the drum and the tambourine. Divide the class into singers and recorder players. Play and sing the song.

B. Enrichment:

1. Create a rhythmic introduction and coda.
2. Have the children create recorder improvisations between repetitions of the song.
3. Teach the bell part.
4. Teach the counting of the dotted quarter and eighth note (♩. ♪) as follows:

   a. Write ♩ ♩ ♩. ♪ | ♩ ♩ ♩ ♩ ‖ on the board.
      (1) Clap this pattern.
      (2) Have the children imitate you.
      (3) Play the melody on your recorder and ask the class how many times this pattern is heard (*three times*).
      (4) Play the melody on your recorder and have the children clap when the pattern occurs.
      (5) Have the children find in their books where this pattern occurs in the melody.
   b. Write the following on the board:

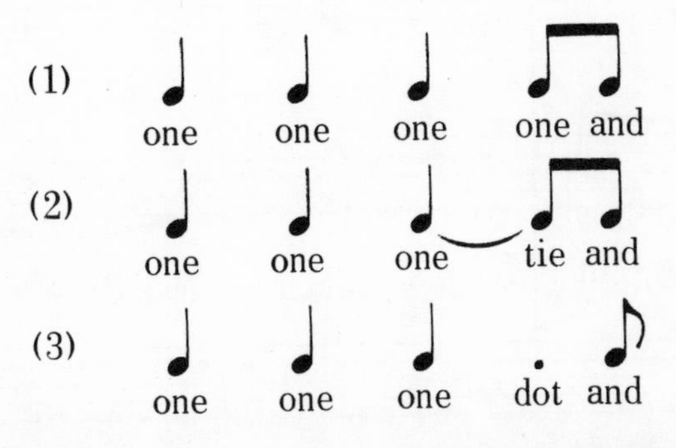

Have the class clap and count one example at a time. Have them make a definite motion to the side, hands clasped together, for the tie and the dot.

The Lone Star Trail

American

LEARNING THE NOTE D

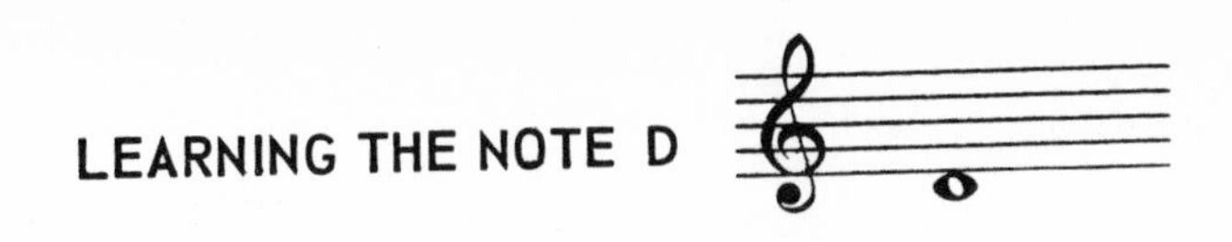

A. Suggested Procedure:

1. Ask the class to play-back on their recorders exactly what you play. Play the following examples, one measure at a time:

2. Write example *e*, above, on the board.
   a. Have the children identify the note names.
   b. Show the recorder fingering for the low "D".
   c. Have the class play this ostinato pattern on their recorders as you sing *The Lone Star Trail*.
3. Ask the children to look at the bell part and identify the note names.
4. Ask for several volunteers to play the bell part.
5. Select one child to play the bells as the class plays the recorder part. When the rhythm of the two parts is well established, you sing the song.
6. Teach the words and have the class sing the song.
7. Clap the triangle part (♩ ♫).
8. Play and sing the complete orchestration.

B. Enrichment:

1. Experiment with rhythm instruments to create the effect of horses trotting slowly.

2. Encourage rhythmic improvisation between repetitions of the song.

3. Create a recorder ostinato using various combinations of the notes "G", "E", "D".

4. Create a rhythmic introduction.

5. Have the children sing the recorder part on *oo* as a second voice part.

6. Sing the song as a two-part round with the voices entering two measures apart.

Alouette

French-Canadian
Recorder
Recorder and/or Voice (Melody)
Bells
Tone Block
Drum
A - lou - et - te, pret- ty A - lou- et - te, A - lou - et - te,
I'll be watch-ing you. I will pluck your feath-er'd head, I will pluck your feath-er'd head,
Lit- tle head, lit - tle head, A-lou-ette, A-lou-ette, Ah! A - lou - et - te,
pret - ty A - lou - et - te, A - lou - et - te, I'll be watch - ing you.

FURTHER EXPERIENCE WITH THE NOTE D

A. Suggested Procedure:

1. Write ♩ ♩ 𝅗𝅥 on the board. Have the children establish a steady clapping of this rhythmic pattern as you play the song on your recorder.

2. Have the children open their books and tell you which four measures of the recorder part are exactly alike (*first and last four measures*).

3. Identify the note names for the first four measures of the recorder part. Have the class play this on their recorders.

4. Sing the entire song as the children play only the first and last four measures of the recorder part.

5. Have the class clap-back measures 5–9 of the recorder part. Direct their attention to the notation of this rhythm. Have several volunteers play measures 5–9 on their recorders.

6. Have the children play the entire recorder part as you sing the song.

7. Have the class sing the song.

8. Teach the bell part in a similar manner as suggested for the recorder. Divide the class into singers, recorder players, and bell players. Play and sing the song.

B. Enrichment:

1. Encourage the children to create rhythmic and melodic improvisations between repetitions of the song.

2. Create a movement pattern to accompany the singing and the playing.

3. Teach the percussion part.

4. Have the children sing either the recorder part or the bell part as a second part to the song.

5. Have the children play the melody on their recorders with or without music.

6. Have the children clap the ♩. ♪ pattern as suggested for *Oh, Susanna.*

7. Have the children play the melodies of *Looby Lou* and *Angel Band* on their recorders.

Hush, Little Baby

American

FURTHER EXPERIENCE WITH THE NOTE D

A. Suggested Procedure:

1. Write the following on a large cardboard or the blackboard:

   a.

   b. (Ostinato)

   (1) Divide the class. Have one group clap and count example *a.* as the second group claps example *b.* Establish two measures of *b.* as an introduction and then cue *a.* clappers to start.

   (2) Explain to the children that line *a.* is the rhythm of a song. Ask if anyone can tell you the name of the song. If they have difficulty, hum the first measure and continue the word rhythms by clapping.

2. Teach the song. Have the children sing the song as you clap

3. Have the children identify the note names for the first four measures of the recorder part.

4. Ask for several volunteers to play the recorder part. Then have the entire class play the recorder part.

5. Divide the class. Have one group play the recorder part while the other group sings and claps.

6. Teach the top bell part.

7. Write on the board to clarify the melodic pattern for the lower bell part.

8. Have several children play the two bell parts.

9. Combine all the parts. Play and sing the song.

B. Enrichment:

1. Have the children play the entire orchestration as a recorder quartet with percussion accompaniment.

2. Have the children sing on *oo* either the recorder part or the bell part with the melody as a two-part singing experience.

3. Teach the percussion accompaniment.

4. Have the children play the melodies of *Old Brass Wagon*, *A Hole in the Bucket*, and *Turn the Glasses Over* on their recorders.

Row, Row, Row Your Boat

American

LEARNING THE NOTE C

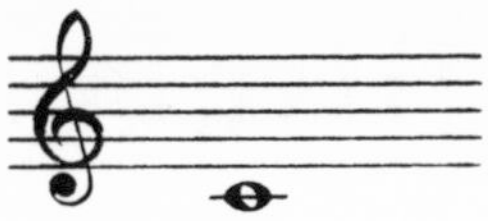

A. Suggested Procedure:

1. Sing the song with the children.

2. Write [C on staff] on the board. Tell the children this note is "C". (It is the lowest note on the recorder and every hole must be covered. It is important that the children play *very softly.*)

3. Write ♩ ♪♩ ♪ on the board. Remind the children that this is counted ♩ ♪♩ ♪ tri - pl - ty tri - pl - ty

   Have the class clap this pattern as an accompaniment to their singing.

4. Have the children play the low "C" on their recorders in a steady ♩. rhythm as you sing the melody.

5. Have the children identify the note names of the bell part.

6. Ask for several volunteers to play the bell part on the bells as the other children play the bell part on their recorders.

7. Divide the class into singers, recorder players and bell players. The recorder and bell players should play the bell part as the singers sing the melody and clap ♩ ♪♩ ♪

8. Ask the children to clap and count the rhythm of the recorder part.

9. Have the children echo your playing: A. B.

10. Ask for several volunteers to play the recorder part.

11. Divide the class. Play and sing the song.

B. Enrichment:

1. Encourage the children to play the melody on their recorders with or without music.

2. Play the entire piece as a recorder trio with the percussion accompaniment.

3. Play the composition as a four-part round on recorders starting two measures apart.

4. Create an introduction, interlude, and coda for rhythm instruments.

5. Teach the percussion parts.

The Marines' Hymn

FURTHER EXPERIENCE WITH NOTE C

A. Suggested Procedure:

1. Write the following on the board:

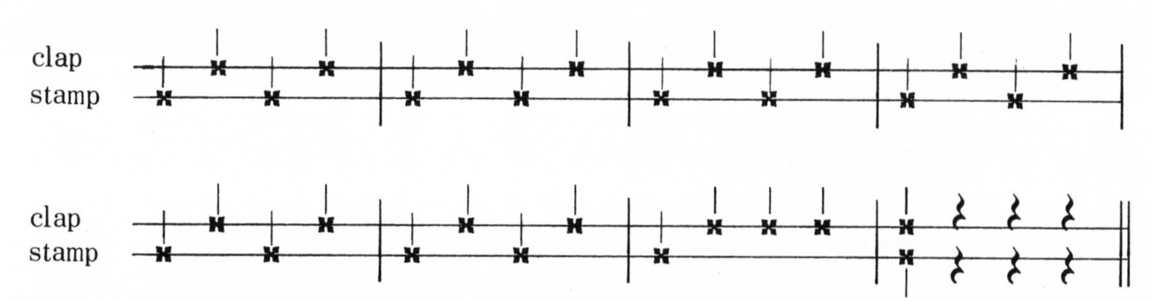

Select one child to point to the notes as the class stamps and claps.

2. You sing the song as the class stamps and claps the rhythm.
3. Teach the song, phrase by phrase, with stamping and clapping.
4. Write the following on the board or on a large cardboard:

   a. Ask the children to clap and count the rhythm. The children should be aware of the repeat signs and the first and second endings.
   b. Have the class identify the notes and finger them on their recorders.
   c. Ask for several volunteers to play the example on their recorders.
   d. Have the entire class play the example.
   e. Ask the children to open their books and find where this example occurs in the recorder part (*first and last eight measures*). Review AABA form.
5. Divide the class into singers and recorder players. Have the singers sing the entire song as the recorder players play only the first and last eight measures. Play and sing the song with stamping and clapping accompaniment.
6. Ask for several volunteers to play the entire recorder part. Then have the class play the entire recorder part.
7. Teach the bell part as suggested above for the recorder.

B. Enrichment:

1. Encourage the children to play the melody on their recorders without music as an ear training experience.
2. Teach the percussion parts.
3. Have the class create a rhythmic introduction, interlude, and coda.
4. Have the children play the song as a recorder trio with percussion accompaniment.
5. Have the children create marching patterns to accompany the singing and playing.
6. Have the children play the melodies of *Swing Low* and *Sleep, Baby, Sleep* on their recorders.

Are You Sleeping?

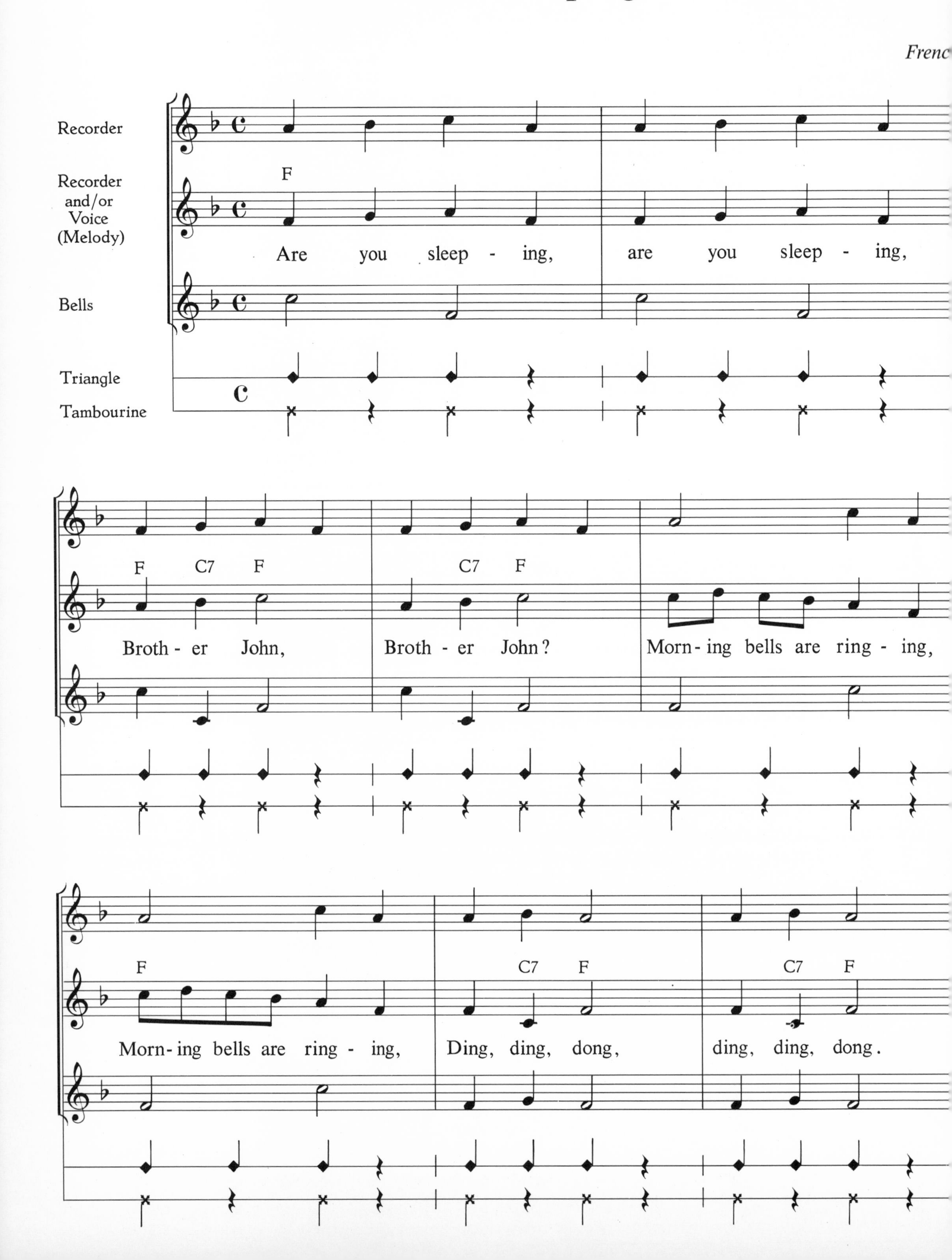

LEARNING THE NOTE B♭

A. Suggested Procedure:

1. Have the children echo:

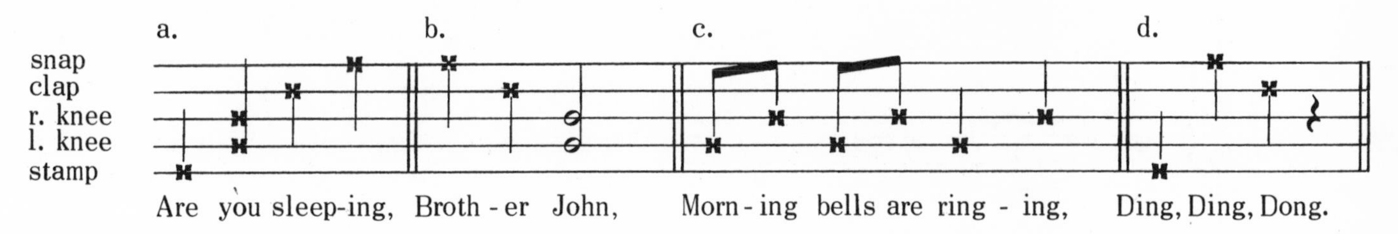

2. Have the children sing-back:

3. Have the children sing and clap the song in its entirety, or phrase by phrase, combining 1 and 2, above.
4. Have the children play-back on their recorders:

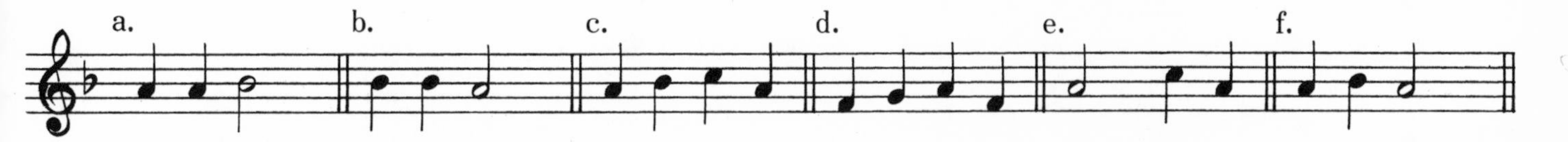

5. Have the children identify the note names of the recorder part. Focus attention on the "B♭" and show the recorder fingering for this note.
6. Ask for several volunteers to play the recorder part.
7. Divide the class into singers and recorder players. Play and sing the song and use the patchen accompaniment above (1).

B. Enrichment:

1. Teach the bell part.
2. Teach the children to play the melody on their recorders.
3. Divide the class for two-part recorder playing (recorder part and melody line).
4. Teach the percussion part.
5. Create rhythmic improvisations for an introduction, interlude, and coda.
6. You may relate the children's clapping and counting of the note values to a time and space relationship as:

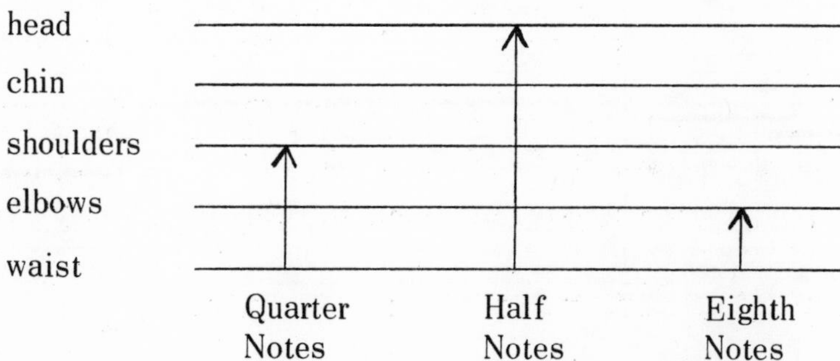

(Note: The objective is to physically demonstrate the length in space of the different note values.)

Polly Wolly Doodle
America
Recorder
Recorder and/or Voice (Melody)
Bells
Tone Block
Drum
Oh, I went down South for to see my Sal, Sing-ing Pol-ly-wol-ly-doo-dle all the
day; My Sal-ly am a spun-ky girl, Sing-ing Pol-ly-wol-ly-doo-dle all the
day. Fare thee well, fare thee well, Fare thee well my fair-y fay, For I'n
going to Loui-si-a-na, For to see my Su-sy-an-na, Sing-ing Pol-ly-wol-ly-doo-dle all the day.

FURTHER EXPERIENCE WITH THE NOTE B♭ 

Children should know this song before this experience is introduced.

A. Suggested Procedure:

1. Write clap stamp on the board. Have the class stamp and clap the rhythm as you play the recorder part.
2. Have the children follow the recorder part as you play. Stop several times in different places. Have the children name the note on which you stopped. Do this several times.
3. Have the children sing the recorder part.
4. Divide the class. Have one group sing the melody while the other group sings the recorder part.
5. Have the children rest the recorder mouthpiece on their chins as they identify and finger the notes of the recorder part.
6. Have the children play the recorder part.
7. Divide the class into singers and recorder players. Have the children play and sing the song as they stamp and clap while you play the bell part.
8. Have the children sing the bell part.
9. Ask for several volunteers to play the bell part.
10. Have the class play and sing the complete orchestration.

B. Enrichment:

1. Have the children play the melody on their recorders.
2. Use one or all of the following patchen patterns in a variety of combinations as an accompaniment to the singing.

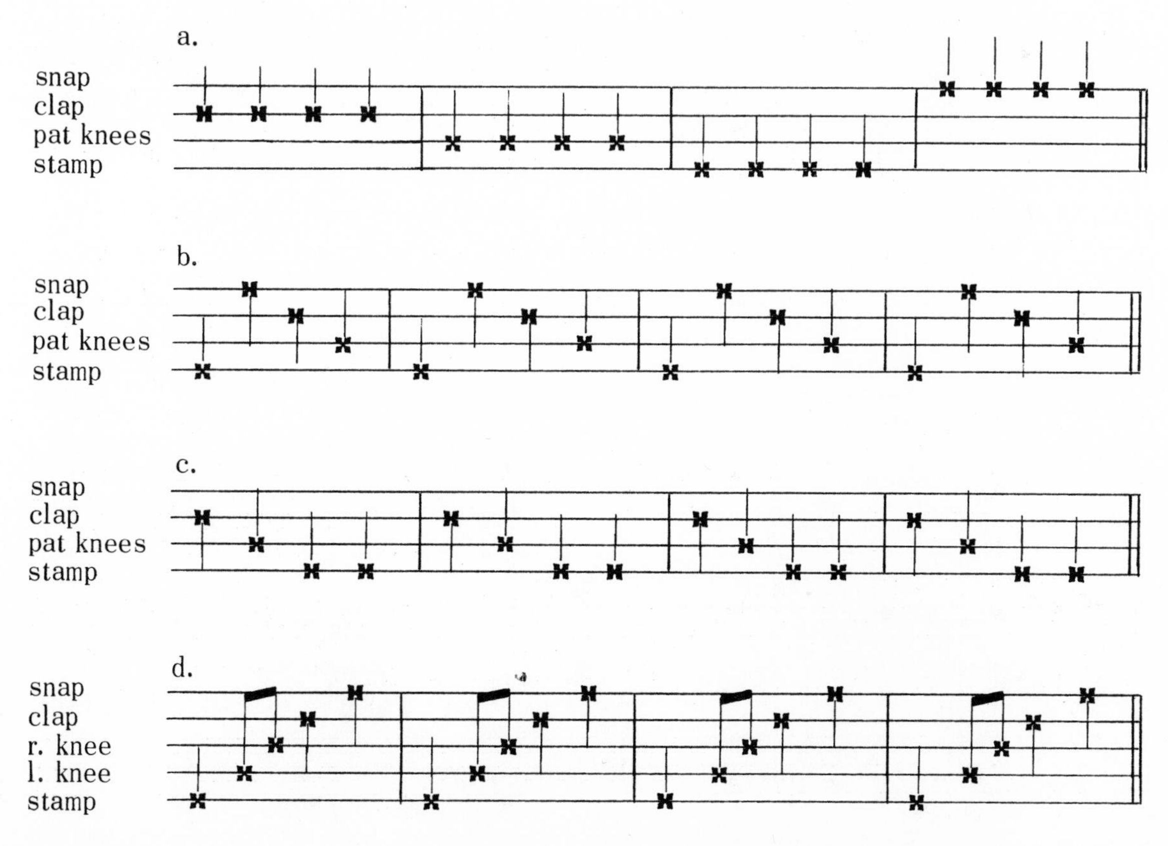

3. Have the children play the melody of *Skip To My Lou* on their recorders.

Chorale

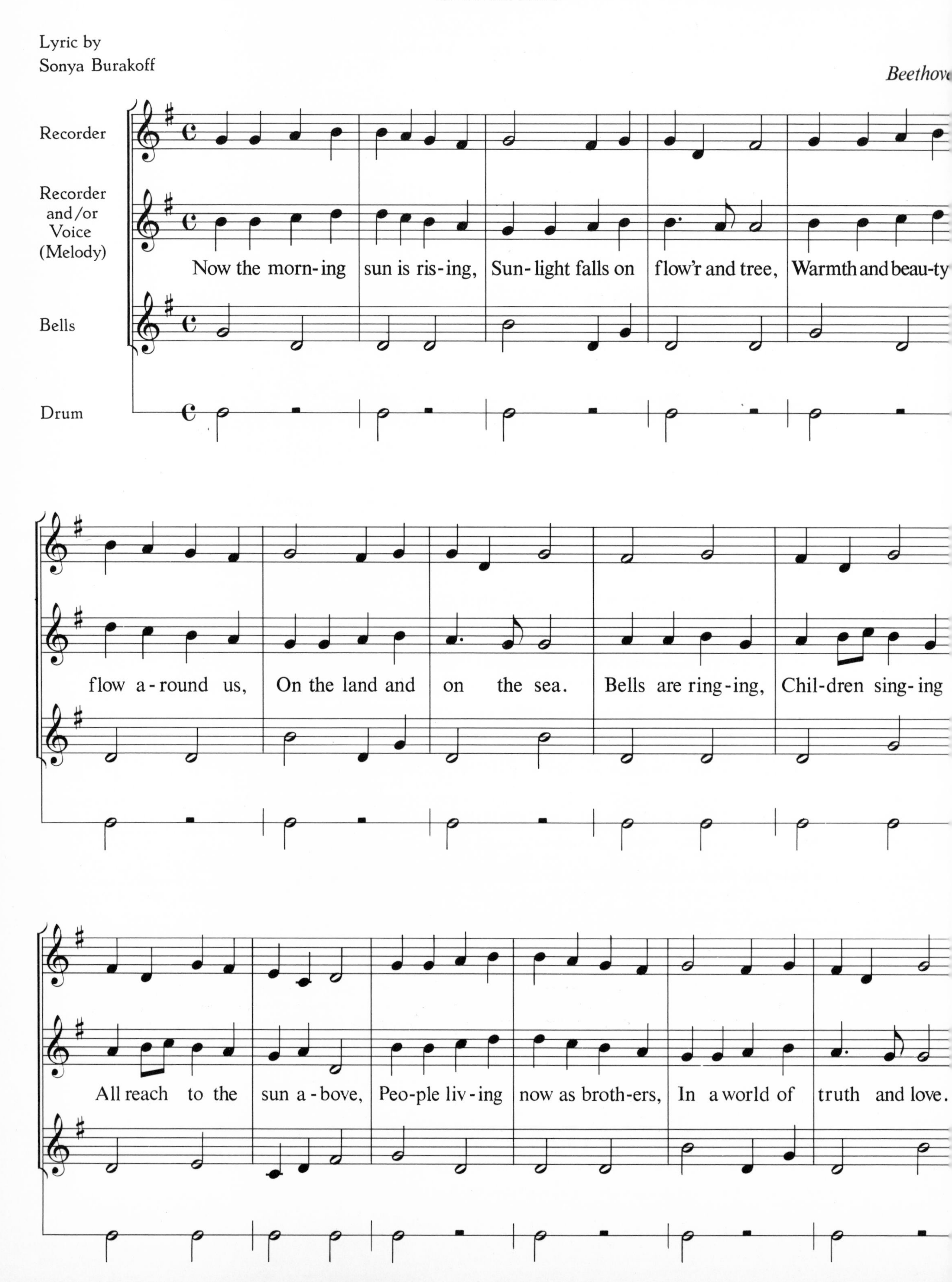
Lyric by
Sonya Burakoff
Beethov
Recorder
Recorder and/or Voice (Melody)
Bells
Drum
Now the morn-ing sun is ris-ing, Sun-light falls on flow'r and tree, Warmth and beau-ty
flow a-round us, On the land and on the sea. Bells are ring-ing, Chil-dren sing-ing
All reach to the sun a-bove, Peo-ple liv-ing now as broth-ers, In a world of truth and love.

LEARNING THE NOTE F♯

A. Suggested Procedure:

1. Write  on the board. Tell the children this is "F♯" and show them the recorder fingering for this note.
2. Ask the children to tell you how many "F♯'s" appear in the recorder part.
3. Have the children identify the note names and finger them on their recorders for the first four measures of the recorder part.
4. Have the class play the first four measures on their recorders.
5. Guide the children to discover the musical form AABA for the recorder part.
6. Sing the entire song as the children play the A sections of the recorder part.
7. Have the children learn the B section of the recorder part.
8. Have the class play the entire recorder part as you sing the melody.
9. Teach the children the song. Show the melodic direction by using your hands or hand signals.
10. Have the children sing the song with words.
11. Divide the class into singers and recorder players. Play and sing the song.
12. Teach the bell part and emphasize AABA form.
13. Add the percussion instruments. Combine all the parts. Play and sing the complete orchestration.

B. Enrichment:

1. Have the class listen to the fourth movement of Beethoven's *Ninth Symphony*.
2. Teach the class to play the melody on their recorders.

Billy Boy

Traditional
Recorder
Voice (Melody)
Bells
Tone Block
Drum
D
Oh, where have you been, Bil - ly Boy, Bil - ly Boy, Oh,
D
A7
where have you been, charm-ing Bil- ly? I have been to seek a wife, She's the
D
A7
D
joy of my life, She's a young thing and can-not leave her moth-er.

FURTHER EXPERIENCE WITH F♯

A. Suggested Procedure:

1. Teach the children to sing the song.

2. Write 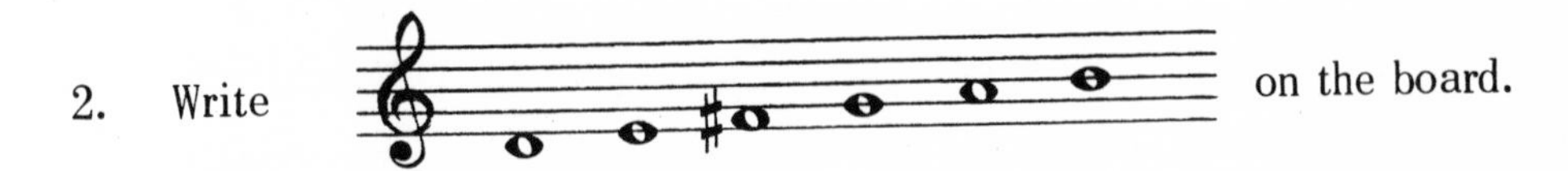 on the board.

   a. Have the children play their recorders as you point to the notes. Point to the notes in the sequence and the rhythm in which they appear in the recorder part.

   b. Divide the class into singers and recorder players. Have the recorder players play the notes you point to (recorder part) while the singers sing the melody.

3. Have the children open their books and identify and finger the notes of the recorder part.

4. Have the children play the recorder part.

5. Have the children sing the song as they clap 𝅗𝅥 ♩ ♩

6. Divide the class into singers and recorder players. Play and sing the song with the clapping accompaniment.

7. Have the children sing the bell part and clap the accompaniment as you direct them with hand signals.

8. Divide the class. Have one group sing the melody. Have the other group sing the bell part as you direct them with hand signals.

9. Ask for several volunteers to play the bell part.

10. Combine all the parts. Play and sing the song.

B. Enrichment:

1. Have the children improvise on their recorders between repetitions of the song. Use only the notes "D", "E", "F♯".

2. Create an introduction and coda for rhythm instruments or recorders.

3. Teach the autoharp accompaniment.

4. Teach the percussion part and encourage the children to experiment with other rhythmic patterns and instruments.

Sweet Betsy from Pike

American

LEARNING THE NOTE C♯

A. Suggested Procedure:

1. Guide the children to discover that the recorder part consists of only five notes.
2. Ask for several volunteers to play the recorder part. Then have the entire class play the recorder part.
3. Write Tambourine / Triangle on the board.

   Have two children play this percussion phrase as an introduction and accompaniment while the class plays the recorder part.
4. Sing the melody. Have the class accompany you with recorders and percussion.
5. Teach the children to sing the melody.
6. Divide the class into percussion players, recorder players, and singers. Play and sing the song.
7. Ask for several volunteers to play the bell part.
8. Play and sing the complete orchestration.
9. Write on the board. Identify this note as "C♯" and show the children the recorder fingering for this note.
10. Write the D Major scale on the board:

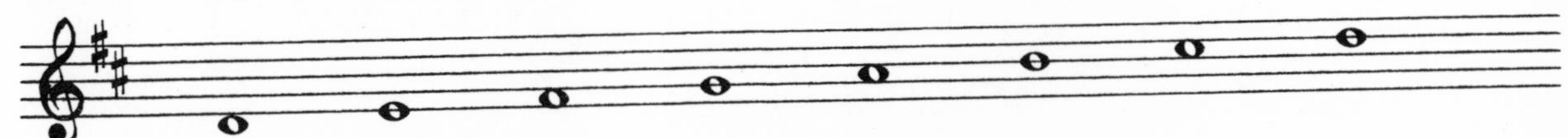

    a. Have the children play the scale.

    b. Have the children play their recorders as you point to the notes. Point to the notes in the sequence and the rhythm in which they appear in the melody.
11. Combine all the parts. Play and sing the song. Include a few children who will play the melody on their recorders.

B. Enrichment:

1. Have the children play the recorder part, melody line, and bell part as a recorder trio.
2. Encourage the children to create clapping patterns in 3/4 meter as a rhythmic accompaniment.

Du, du liegst mir im Herzen

English Lyric by
Sonya Burakoff

German

LEARNING THE NOTE F

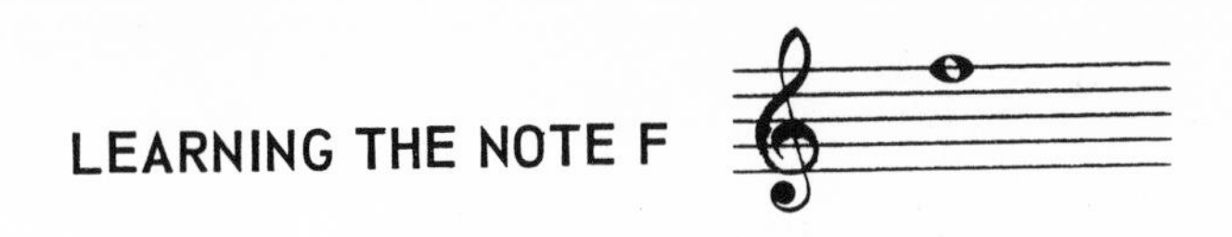

A. Suggested Procedure:

1. Write [staff with note F] on the board. Identify this as "F" and show the recorder fingering.

   Remind the class of the correct way to partially uncover the thumb hole in the back.

2. Have the children play-back the following as a means of developing facility in the use of thumbing:

3. Have the class open their books and play the melody on their recorders. Teach four measures at a time.

4. Divide the class into singers and recorder players. Sing and play the melody.

5. Ask for volunteers to play the recorder part.

6. Divide the class into singers and recorder players. Sing the melody and play the recorder part.

7. Write

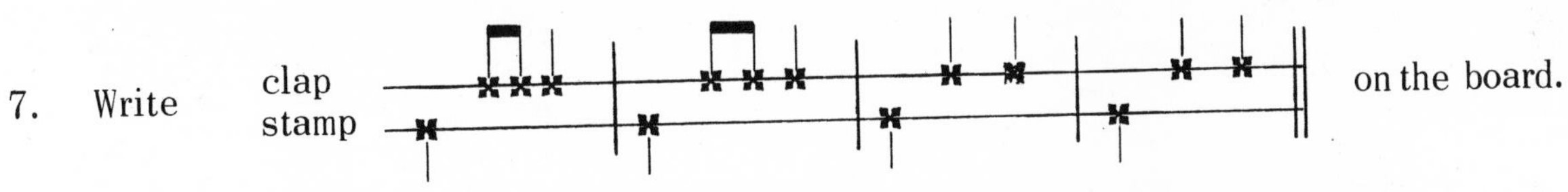

   on the board.

   Have the children stamp and clap this pattern as an accompaniment to singing.

8. Ask for several volunteers to play the bell part.

9. Have the children sing the melody as one child plays the bell part.

10. Teach the percussion part.

11. Combine all the parts. Play and sing the complete orchestration.

B. Enrichment:

1. Create an introduction, interlude, and coda for recorders and percussion.

2. Play all the parts as a recorder trio with percussion accompaniment.

3. Teach the autoharp chording.

4. Teach the children to play the melody of *'Liza Jane* on their recorders.

FINGERING CHART for SOPRANO RECORDER

Two Octaves

	C	C♯ D♭	D	D♯ E♭	E	F	F (German)	F♯	G♭ (German)	G	G♯ A♭	A	A♯ B♭	B
Thumb hole	●	●	●	●	●	●	■	●	■	●	●	●	●	●
Left Hand – 1	●	●	●	●	●	●	■	●	■	●	●	●	●	●
Left Hand – 2	●	●	●	●	●	●	■	●	■	●	●	●		
Left Hand – 3	●	●	●	●	●	●	■	●	■	●			●	
Right Hand – 1	●	●	●	●	●	●	■				●		●	
Right Hand – 2	●	●	●	●	●			●	■		●			
Right Hand – 3	●	●	●	◐*		●		●	■					
Right Hand – 4	●	◐*				●			■					

	C	C♯ D♭	D	D♯ E♭	E	F	F (German)	F♯	G♭ (German)	G	G♯ A♭	A	A♯ B♭	B	C
Thumb hole	●				◓	◓	■	◓	■	◓	◓	◓	◓	◓	◓
Left Hand – 1		●			●	●	■	●	■	●	●	●	●	●	●
Left Hand – 2	●	●	●	●	●	●	■	●	■	●	●	●	●	●	
Left Hand – 3				●	●	●	■	●	■	●					
Right Hand – 1				●	●	●	■				●		●	●	●
Right Hand – 2				●	●			●	■				●	●	●
Right Hand – 3				●		●							●		
Right Hand – 4									■						

ILLUSTRATED BY RAY KOOS

◐ Partly closed hole

● Closed hole

◓ Thumb pressed into thumb-hole

◐* This fingering is for single holed recorders. If yours is a double holed recorder, cover the hole like this....

■ German fingering